THIS PET JOURNAL BELONGS TO

_____

_____

_____

CONTACT DETAILS

_____

_____

_____

_____

DEDICATION

This Dog Log Journal book is dedicated to all the dog owners out there who love their dog, want to track their dogs' health and activities, and document their findings in the process.

You are my inspiration for producing books and I'm honored to be a part of keeping all of your Dog Health notes and records organized.

This journal notebook will help you record your details about your precious pet.

Thoughtfully put together with these sections to record:
Pet Details Page, Bath & Grooming, Vaccination, Surgery History, Veterinarian Appointments, and Daily Activities.

HOW TO USE THIS BOOK

The purpose of this book is to keep all of your Dog Health & Activities notes all in one place. It will help keep you organized.

This Dog Log Journal will allow you to accurately document every detail about your dog or puppy. It's a great way to chart your course through a healthy pet.

Here are examples of the prompts for you to fill in and write about your experience in this book:

1. **Pet Details Page** - Write Pet Name, Date of Birth, Owner's Name, Address, Phone Number, Vet's Name & Contact, Allergies & Conditions.
2. **Bath & Grooming** - Track when they get a bath & groomed, date, time, age, weight & procedure.
3. **Vaccination** - Record Vaccinations and Immunization, Date & Age.
4. **Surgery History** - Log any surgeries they have, date & age.
5. **Veterinarian Appointments** - For writing each vet visit, vet name, time, date, and age.
6. **Daily Activities** - Track their daily activities each day for exercise, water, food & meals, medication, and other notes.

Enjoy!

PET NAME

_____

DATE OF BIRTH

_____

OWNER/S

_____

_____

ADDRESS

_____

PHONE NUMBER

_____

VET'S NAME

_____

CONTACT DETAILS

_____

_____

ALLERGIES & MEDICAL CONDITIONS

_____

_____

_____

_____

_____

YEARLY TRACKER

	BATH DAY	GROOMING DAY	WEIGHT
J			
F			
M			
A			
M			
J			
J			
A			
S			
O			
N			
D			

PET VACCINE INFORMATION

VACCINE NAME	DATE	AGE

PET SURGERY INFORMATION

SURGERY	DATE	AGE

VET APPOINTMENT INFORMATION

VET	TIME	DATE	AGE

VET APPOINTMENT INFORMATION

VET	TIME	DATE	AGE

PET GROOMING INFORMATION

PROCEDURE	TIME	DATE	AGE

PET GROOMING INFORMATION

PROCEDURE	TIME	DATE	AGE

WEEKLY TRACKER

MONTH: **WEEK:**

	EXERCISE	WATER	FOOD	MEDICATION	OTHER
MON					
TUE					
WED					
THU					
FRI					
SAT					
SUN					

WEEKLY TRACKER

MONTH: **WEEK:**

	EXERCISE	WATER	FOOD	MEDICATION	OTHER
MON					
TUE					
WED					
THU					
FRI					
SAT					
SUN					

WEEKLY TRACKER

MONTH: **WEEK:**

	EXERCISE	WATER	FOOD	MEDICATION	OTHER
MON					
TUE					
WED					
THU					
FRI					
SAT					
SUN					

WEEKLY TRACKER

MONTH: **WEEK:**

	EXERCISE	WATER	FOOD	MEDICATION	OTHER
MON					
TUE					
WED					
THU					
FRI					
SAT					
SUN					

WEEKLY TRACKER

MONTH: **WEEK:**

	EXERCISE	WATER	FOOD	MEDICATION	OTHER
MON					
TUE					
WED					
THU					
FRI					
SAT					
SUN					

WEEKLY TRACKER

MONTH: **WEEK:**

	EXERCISE	WATER	FOOD	MEDICATION	OTHER
MON					
TUE					
WED					
THU					
FRI					
SAT					
SUN					

WEEKLY TRACKER

MONTH: **WEEK:**

	EXERCISE	WATER	FOOD	MEDICATION	OTHER
MON					
TUE					
WED					
THU					
FRI					
SAT					
SUN					

WEEKLY TRACKER

MONTH: **WEEK:**

	EXERCISE	WATER	FOOD	MEDICATION	OTHER
MON					
TUE					
WED					
THU					
FRI					
SAT					
SUN					

WEEKLY TRACKER

MONTH: **WEEK:**

	EXERCISE	WATER	FOOD	MEDICATION	OTHER
MON					
TUE					
WED					
THU					
FRI					
SAT					
SUN					

WEEKLY TRACKER

MONTH: **WEEK:**

	EXERCISE	WATER	FOOD	MEDICATION	OTHER
MON					
TUE					
WED					
THU					
FRI					
SAT					
SUN					

WEEKLY TRACKER

MONTH: **WEEK:**

	EXERCISE	WATER	FOOD	MEDICATION	OTHER
MON					
TUE					
WED					
THU					
FRI					
SAT					
SUN					

WEEKLY TRACKER

MONTH: **WEEK:**

	EXERCISE	WATER	FOOD	MEDICATION	OTHER
MON					
TUE					
WED					
THU					
FRI					
SAT					
SUN					

WEEKLY TRACKER

MONTH: **WEEK:**

	EXERCISE	WATER	FOOD	MEDICATION	OTHER
MON					
TUE					
WED					
THU					
FRI					
SAT					
SUN					

WEEKLY TRACKER

MONTH: **WEEK:**

	EXERCISE	WATER	FOOD	MEDICATION	OTHER
MON					
TUE					
WED					
THU					
FRI					
SAT					
SUN					

WEEKLY TRACKER

MONTH: **WEEK:**

	EXERCISE	WATER	FOOD	MEDICATION	OTHER
MON					
TUE					
WED					
THU					
FRI					
SAT					
SUN					

WEEKLY TRACKER

MONTH: **WEEK:**

	EXERCISE	WATER	FOOD	MEDICATION	OTHER
MON					
TUE					
WED					
THU					
FRI					
SAT					
SUN					

WEEKLY TRACKER

MONTH: **WEEK:**

	EXERCISE	WATER	FOOD	MEDICATION	OTHER
MON					
TUE					
WED					
THU					
FRI					
SAT					
SUN					

WEEKLY TRACKER

MONTH: **WEEK:**

	EXERCISE	WATER	FOOD	MEDICATION	OTHER
MON					
TUE					
WED					
THU					
FRI					
SAT					
SUN					

WEEKLY TRACKER

MONTH: **WEEK:**

	EXERCISE	WATER	FOOD	MEDICATION	OTHER
MON					
TUE					
WED					
THU					
FRI					
SAT					
SUN					

WEEKLY TRACKER

MONTH: **WEEK:**

	EXERCISE	WATER	FOOD	MEDICATION	OTHER
MON					
TUE					
WED					
THU					
FRI					
SAT					
SUN					

WEEKLY TRACKER

MONTH: **WEEK:**

	EXERCISE	WATER	FOOD	MEDICATION	OTHER
MON					
TUE					
WED					
THU					
FRI					
SAT					
SUN					

WEEKLY TRACKER

MONTH: **WEEK:**

	EXERCISE	WATER	FOOD	MEDICATION	OTHER
MON					
TUE					
WED					
THU					
FRI					
SAT					
SUN					

WEEKLY TRACKER

MONTH: **WEEK:**

	EXERCISE	WATER	FOOD	MEDICATION	OTHER
MON					
TUE					
WED					
THU					
FRI					
SAT					
SUN					

WEEKLY TRACKER

MONTH: **WEEK:**

	EXERCISE	WATER	FOOD	MEDICATION	OTHER
MON					
TUE					
WED					
THU					
FRI					
SAT					
SUN					

WEEKLY TRACKER

MONTH: **WEEK:**

	EXERCISE	WATER	FOOD	MEDICATION	OTHER
MON					
TUE					
WED					
THU					
FRI					
SAT					
SUN					

WEEKLY TRACKER

MONTH:　　　　　　　　**WEEK:**

	EXERCISE	WATER	FOOD	MEDICATION	OTHER
MON					
TUE					
WED					
THU					
FRI					
SAT					
SUN					

WEEKLY TRACKER

MONTH: **WEEK:**

	EXERCISE	WATER	FOOD	MEDICATION	OTHER
MON					
TUE					
WED					
THU					
FRI					
SAT					
SUN					

WEEKLY TRACKER

MONTH: **WEEK:**

	EXERCISE	WATER	FOOD	MEDICATION	OTHER
MON					
TUE					
WED					
THU					
FRI					
SAT					
SUN					

WEEKLY TRACKER

MONTH: **WEEK:**

	EXERCISE	WATER	FOOD	MEDICATION	OTHER
MON					
TUE					
WED					
THU					
FRI					
SAT					
SUN					

WEEKLY TRACKER

MONTH: **WEEK:**

	EXERCISE	WATER	FOOD	MEDICATION	OTHER
MON					
TUE					
WED					
THU					
FRI					
SAT					
SUN					

WEEKLY TRACKER

MONTH: **WEEK:**

	EXERCISE	WATER	FOOD	MEDICATION	OTHER
MON					
TUE					
WED					
THU					
FRI					
SAT					
SUN					

WEEKLY TRACKER

MONTH: **WEEK:**

	EXERCISE	WATER	FOOD	MEDICATION	OTHER
MON					
TUE					
WED					
THU					
FRI					
SAT					
SUN					

WEEKLY TRACKER

MONTH: **WEEK:**

	EXERCISE	WATER	FOOD	MEDICATION	OTHER
MON					
TUE					
WED					
THU					
FRI					
SAT					
SUN					

WEEKLY TRACKER

MONTH: WEEK:

	EXERCISE	WATER	FOOD	MEDICATION	OTHER
MON					
TUE					
WED					
THU					
FRI					
SAT					
SUN					

WEEKLY TRACKER

MONTH: **WEEK:**

	EXERCISE	WATER	FOOD	MEDICATION	OTHER
MON					
TUE					
WED					
THU					
FRI					
SAT					
SUN					

WEEKLY TRACKER

MONTH: WEEK:

	EXERCISE	WATER	FOOD	MEDICATION	OTHER
MON					
TUE					
WED					
THU					
FRI					
SAT					
SUN					

WEEKLY TRACKER

MONTH: **WEEK:**

	EXERCISE	WATER	FOOD	MEDICATION	OTHER
MON					
TUE					
WED					
THU					
FRI					
SAT					
SUN					

WEEKLY TRACKER

MONTH: **WEEK:**

	EXERCISE	WATER	FOOD	MEDICATION	OTHER
MON					
TUE					
WED					
THU					
FRI					
SAT					
SUN					

WEEKLY TRACKER

MONTH: **WEEK:**

	EXERCISE	WATER	FOOD	MEDICATION	OTHER
MON					
TUE					
WED					
THU					
FRI					
SAT					
SUN					

WEEKLY TRACKER

MONTH:　　　　　　　　**WEEK:**

	EXERCISE	WATER	FOOD	MEDICATION	OTHER
MON					
TUE					
WED					
THU					
FRI					
SAT					
SUN					

WEEKLY TRACKER

MONTH: **WEEK:**

	EXERCISE	WATER	FOOD	MEDICATION	OTHER
MON					
TUE					
WED					
THU					
FRI					
SAT					
SUN					

WEEKLY TRACKER

MONTH: **WEEK:**

	EXERCISE	WATER	FOOD	MEDICATION	OTHER
MON					
TUE					
WED					
THU					
FRI					
SAT					
SUN					

WEEKLY TRACKER

MONTH: **WEEK:**

	EXERCISE	WATER	FOOD	MEDICATION	OTHER
MON					
TUE					
WED					
THU					
FRI					
SAT					
SUN					

WEEKLY TRACKER

MONTH: **WEEK:**

	EXERCISE	WATER	FOOD	MEDICATION	OTHER
MON					
TUE					
WED					
THU					
FRI					
SAT					
SUN					

WEEKLY TRACKER

MONTH: **WEEK:**

	EXERCISE	WATER	FOOD	MEDICATION	OTHER
MON					
TUE					
WED					
THU					
FRI					
SAT					
SUN					

WEEKLY TRACKER

MONTH: **WEEK:**

	EXERCISE	WATER	FOOD	MEDICATION	OTHER
MON					
TUE					
WED					
THU					
FRI					
SAT					
SUN					

WEEKLY TRACKER

MONTH: **WEEK:**

	EXERCISE	WATER	FOOD	MEDICATION	OTHER
MON					
TUE					
WED					
THU					
FRI					
SAT					
SUN					

WEEKLY TRACKER

MONTH: **WEEK:**

	EXERCISE	WATER	FOOD	MEDICATION	OTHER
MON					
TUE					
WED					
THU					
FRI					
SAT					
SUN					

WEEKLY TRACKER

MONTH: **WEEK:**

	EXERCISE	WATER	FOOD	MEDICATION	OTHER
MON					
TUE					
WED					
THU					
FRI					
SAT					
SUN					

WEEKLY TRACKER

MONTH: **WEEK:**

	EXERCISE	WATER	FOOD	MEDICATION	OTHER
MON					
TUE					
WED					
THU					
FRI					
SAT					
SUN					

WEEKLY TRACKER

MONTH: **WEEK:**

	EXERCISE	WATER	FOOD	MEDICATION	OTHER
MON					
TUE					
WED					
THU					
FRI					
SAT					
SUN					

WEEKLY TRACKER

MONTH: **WEEK:**

	EXERCISE	WATER	FOOD	MEDICATION	OTHER
MON					
TUE					
WED					
THU					
FRI					
SAT					
SUN					

WEEKLY TRACKER

MONTH: **WEEK:**

	EXERCISE	WATER	FOOD	MEDICATION	OTHER
MON					
TUE					
WED					
THU					
FRI					
SAT					
SUN					

WEEKLY TRACKER

MONTH: **WEEK:**

	EXERCISE	WATER	FOOD	MEDICATION	OTHER
MON					
TUE					
WED					
THU					
FRI					
SAT					
SUN					

WEEKLY TRACKER

MONTH: WEEK:

	EXERCISE	WATER	FOOD	MEDICATION	OTHER
MON					
TUE					
WED					
THU					
FRI					
SAT					
SUN					

WEEKLY TRACKER

MONTH: **WEEK:**

	EXERCISE	WATER	FOOD	MEDICATION	OTHER
MON					
TUE					
WED					
THU					
FRI					
SAT					
SUN					

WEEKLY TRACKER

MONTH: **WEEK:**

	EXERCISE	WATER	FOOD	MEDICATION	OTHER
MON					
TUE					
WED					
THU					
FRI					
SAT					
SUN					

WEEKLY TRACKER

MONTH: **WEEK:**

	EXERCISE	WATER	FOOD	MEDICATION	OTHER
MON					
TUE					
WED					
THU					
FRI					
SAT					
SUN					

WEEKLY TRACKER

MONTH: **WEEK:**

	EXERCISE	WATER	FOOD	MEDICATION	OTHER
MON					
TUE					
WED					
THU					
FRI					
SAT					
SUN					

WEEKLY TRACKER

MONTH: **WEEK:**

	EXERCISE	WATER	FOOD	MEDICATION	OTHER
MON					
TUE					
WED					
THU					
FRI					
SAT					
SUN					

WEEKLY TRACKER

MONTH: **WEEK:**

	EXERCISE	WATER	FOOD	MEDICATION	OTHER
MON					
TUE					
WED					
THU					
FRI					
SAT					
SUN					

WEEKLY TRACKER

MONTH: **WEEK:**

	EXERCISE	WATER	FOOD	MEDICATION	OTHER
MON					
TUE					
WED					
THU					
FRI					
SAT					
SUN					

WEEKLY TRACKER

MONTH:

WEEK:

	EXERCISE	WATER	FOOD	MEDICATION	OTHER
MON					
TUE					
WED					
THU					
FRI					
SAT					
SUN					

WEEKLY TRACKER

MONTH: **WEEK:**

	EXERCISE	WATER	FOOD	MEDICATION	OTHER
MON					
TUE					
WED					
THU					
FRI					
SAT					
SUN					

WEEKLY TRACKER

MONTH: **WEEK:**

	EXERCISE	WATER	FOOD	MEDICATION	OTHER
MON					
TUE					
WED					
THU					
FRI					
SAT					
SUN					

WEEKLY TRACKER

MONTH: **WEEK:**

	EXERCISE	WATER	FOOD	MEDICATION	OTHER
MON					
TUE					
WED					
THU					
FRI					
SAT					
SUN					

WEEKLY TRACKER

MONTH: **WEEK:**

	EXERCISE	WATER	FOOD	MEDICATION	OTHER
MON					
TUE					
WED					
THU					
FRI					
SAT					
SUN					

WEEKLY TRACKER

MONTH: **WEEK:**

	EXERCISE	WATER	FOOD	MEDICATION	OTHER
MON					
TUE					
WED					
THU					
FRI					
SAT					
SUN					

WEEKLY TRACKER

MONTH: **WEEK:**

	EXERCISE	WATER	FOOD	MEDICATION	OTHER
MON					
TUE					
WED					
THU					
FRI					
SAT					
SUN					

WEEKLY TRACKER

MONTH: **WEEK:**

	EXERCISE	WATER	FOOD	MEDICATION	OTHER
MON					
TUE					
WED					
THU					
FRI					
SAT					
SUN					

WEEKLY TRACKER

MONTH: **WEEK:**

	EXERCISE	WATER	FOOD	MEDICATION	OTHER
MON					
TUE					
WED					
THU					
FRI					
SAT					
SUN					

WEEKLY TRACKER

MONTH: **WEEK:**

	EXERCISE	WATER	FOOD	MEDICATION	OTHER
MON					
TUE					
WED					
THU					
FRI					
SAT					
SUN					

WEEKLY TRACKER

MONTH: **WEEK:**

	EXERCISE	WATER	FOOD	MEDICATION	OTHER
MON					
TUE					
WED					
THU					
FRI					
SAT					
SUN					

WEEKLY TRACKER

MONTH:

WEEK:

	EXERCISE	WATER	FOOD	MEDICATION	OTHER
MON					
TUE					
WED					
THU					
FRI					
SAT					
SUN					

WEEKLY TRACKER

MONTH: **WEEK:**

	EXERCISE	WATER	FOOD	MEDICATION	OTHER
MON					
TUE					
WED					
THU					
FRI					
SAT					
SUN					

WEEKLY TRACKER

MONTH: **WEEK:**

	EXERCISE	WATER	FOOD	MEDICATION	OTHER
MON					
TUE					
WED					
THU					
FRI					
SAT					
SUN					

WEEKLY TRACKER

MONTH: **WEEK:**

	EXERCISE	WATER	FOOD	MEDICATION	OTHER
MON					
TUE					
WED					
THU					
FRI					
SAT					
SUN					

WEEKLY TRACKER

MONTH: **WEEK:**

	EXERCISE	WATER	FOOD	MEDICATION	OTHER
MON					
TUE					
WED					
THU					
FRI					
SAT					
SUN					

WEEKLY TRACKER

MONTH: **WEEK:**

	EXERCISE	WATER	FOOD	MEDICATION	OTHER
MON					
TUE					
WED					
THU					
FRI					
SAT					
SUN					

WEEKLY TRACKER

MONTH: **WEEK:**

	EXERCISE	WATER	FOOD	MEDICATION	OTHER
MON					
TUE					
WED					
THU					
FRI					
SAT					
SUN					

WEEKLY TRACKER

MONTH: **WEEK:**

	EXERCISE	WATER	FOOD	MEDICATION	OTHER
MON					
TUE					
WED					
THU					
FRI					
SAT					
SUN					

WEEKLY TRACKER

MONTH: **WEEK:**

	EXERCISE	WATER	FOOD	MEDICATION	OTHER
MON					
TUE					
WED					
THU					
FRI					
SAT					
SUN					

WEEKLY TRACKER

MONTH: **WEEK:**

	EXERCISE	WATER	FOOD	MEDICATION	OTHER
MON					
TUE					
WED					
THU					
FRI					
SAT					
SUN					

WEEKLY TRACKER

MONTH: **WEEK:**

	EXERCISE	WATER	FOOD	MEDICATION	OTHER
MON					
TUE					
WED					
THU					
FRI					
SAT					
SUN					

WEEKLY TRACKER

MONTH: **WEEK:**

	EXERCISE	WATER	FOOD	MEDICATION	OTHER
MON					
TUE					
WED					
THU					
FRI					
SAT					
SUN					

WEEKLY TRACKER

MONTH: **WEEK:**

	EXERCISE	WATER	FOOD	MEDICATION	OTHER
MON					
TUE					
WED					
THU					
FRI					
SAT					
SUN					

WEEKLY TRACKER

MONTH: **WEEK:**

	EXERCISE	WATER	FOOD	MEDICATION	OTHER
MON					
TUE					
WED					
THU					
FRI					
SAT					
SUN					

WEEKLY TRACKER

MONTH: **WEEK:**

	EXERCISE	WATER	FOOD	MEDICATION	OTHER
MON					
TUE					
WED					
THU					
FRI					
SAT					
SUN					

WEEKLY TRACKER

MONTH: **WEEK:**

	EXERCISE	WATER	FOOD	MEDICATION	OTHER
MON					
TUE					
WED					
THU					
FRI					
SAT					
SUN					

WEEKLY TRACKER

MONTH: **WEEK:**

	EXERCISE	WATER	FOOD	MEDICATION	OTHER
MON					
TUE					
WED					
THU					
FRI					
SAT					
SUN					

WEEKLY TRACKER

MONTH: **WEEK:**

	EXERCISE	WATER	FOOD	MEDICATION	OTHER
MON					
TUE					
WED					
THU					
FRI					
SAT					
SUN					

www.ingramcontent.com/pod-product-compliance
Lightning Source LLC
Chambersburg PA
CBHW051032030426
42336CB00015B/2838

9 781649 441706